BLACK BI

a triumph

What's On in London

"delightful"

Benedict Nightingale, *The Times*

"as acute as an Alan Bennett but shot with an exotic tenderness all of its own"

Time Out

"A vivid, funny, touching yet uncloying account of the tears and laughter of an extraordinary experience"

Godfrey Smith, *The Sunday Times*

"An elegant tale of playing Chekhov to the natives. Caroline Blakiston's eye for detail and her skill conjuring the mood and atmosphere of another climate and culture is wonderfully evocative"

David Benedict, *The Independent*

"The show gripped one throughout. It made me laugh and it made me cry. It also taught one a lot. I'm not sure you can ask for much more from a piece of theatre."

Michael Attenborough

"The one-woman show, Black Bread and Cucumber, is not only about Russia, about Caroline's guest appearance as Charlotta in The Cherry Orchard in Taganrog and at the Moscow Art Theatre, it is also about fellow feeling among human beings in general. It is performed with so much life, with great taste, with marvellous humour and lyricism. Wonderful!"

Oleg Yefremov, former Artistic Director, Moscow Art Theatre

BLACK BREAD & CUCUMBER

a true story

by

CAROLINE BLAKISTON

UPSTAGE

First published in England in July 2011
by Upstage (an imprint of Classic TV Press)
103 High Street, Cherry Hinton, Cambridge, CB1 9LU, England
e: classictvpress@live.co.uk
w: http://www.classictvpress.co.uk/

ISBN: 978-0-9561000-5-4 (paperback)

Internal design and layout by Classic TV Press

Printed and bound in Great Britain by
CPI Antony Rowe, Chippenham and Eastbourne

1 2 3 4 5 6 7 8 9 10 11 12 13 14 15

British Library Cataloguing in Publication Data
A catalogue record for this book is available from the British Library

For Adam and Charlotte

ACKNOWLEDGMENTS

My first wish is to thank Layla Alexander whose imaginative flair made the vital connection between me and those in Russia who were willing to take a chance on a stranger.

Then Ian McDiarmid and Jonathan Kent gave me a slot at the Almeida Theatre to put out some early halting sentences. Jenny Topper at Hampstead Theatre took it forward by suggesting that Mark Thomson could alter my feelings of helplessness in the face of the huge amount of material I had both written into notebooks and spoken onto a cassette recorder while I was in Russia. He did so, kindly and efficiently. Michael Frayn generously allowed me to use his translation of the touching lines Simeonov-Pishchik speaks when he discovers in Act IV that his beloved friends are leaving for ever.

I practised my lines loudly as I learned them, striding around Richmond Park. The deer scarcely raised their heads. When I knew the text better I came closer to home in the walled garden of Fulham Palace Gardens. The first human to whom I spoke it was my trusted old friend Edward Petherbridge, in his sitting room. I was wearing his tailcoat. When it was done he made me tea. His pinpoint empathetic comments have led me to use him as a sounding board for my work ever since.

Arthur Cox, an encyclopaedia of melodies, made perfect choices of music for me. Ann Queensberry took my typed pages and transferred them to floppy disc. She also introduced me to Upstage, the publishers of this book. It was Sam Walters at the Orange Tree Theatre who hosted the first London appearances of Black Bread & Cucumber. A Sunday matinee and evening shot. Auriol Smith convinced me that the title I chose was the right one.

Roy and Hilary King of the Red Pear Theatre in Antibes sponsored my first central London run at the Jermyn Street Theatre, and Penny Horner, doyenne of that venue, has given me a home there twice since.

Finally, and most recently, Jill Hyem of TV's Tenko and many other dramas, Anne Hogben of the Writers Guild and Tom Erhardt of Casarotto Ramsay and Associates, with light touch and plenty of encouragement helped me to feel confident to go into print with my extraordinary new friends and business partners, Andy and Marisa Priestner of Upstage. We seem to agree about everything.

Spassibo, everyone.

CONTENTS

FOREWORD

My Russian Illness

It may have begun in 1932 when, during a tourist trip to the USSR, my parents discovered that they were expecting me. So I was in Russia before I was born.

They were intellectuals; my father, an archivist at the Public Record Office, son of an Anglican clergyman, writer, leaned to the Right; my mother, lofty in her Liberal lineage, writer, always voted Labour, she said. When they married in 1930 they bought and lived in a tall house in a Chelsea Square where my mother died in her 92nd year.

I was first conscious of the electrifying effect the words RUSSIAN and MUSCOVITE were to have on me when at sixteen I performed a humourless Berowne in a school production of Love's Labour's Lost. The visiting male director struggled to help me; "Berowne's witty, like Benedick." Who? However, I felt an unusual charge of excitement as Berowne, Longaville and Dumaine made our ridiculous bearded way onto the open air stage and spoke the few Russian-accented lines. Something was going on. An intriguing foreign door was opening inside me. The unaccountable yearning had started and I liked it.

I read Crime and Punishment by Dostoyevsky. A knockout. Neither academic nor mature enough to go to University and already consumed with the need to act, which I put on hold, I had an unexpected chance to go to New York for the year 1953-4 as personal assistant to the wife of the British Ambassador to the UN. I signed the most junior version of The Official Secrets Act and was required to remember, amongst other things, the identities and titles of whomsoever the Ambassadress met. I found that the names of the Russian Delegates were the easiest to learn and I practised them out loud when I was alone. At a party in the garden of the official residence on the banks of the Hudson River one sunny day I found myself welcoming the Soviet Foreign Minister, Andrey Vyshinsky, at the front door. He smilingly taught me my first word of Russian:

1

'jarka' (hot). That year I read War and Peace by Tolstoy. I was a goner.

On my return from the USA I entered RADA which led to experience in repertory companies and, in time, West End plays. I married Russell Hunter, the best and bravest Shakespearean clown I've encountered. With two young children I tried to choose only TV and film jobs for some years, so that I might be at home to put them to bed; it didn't always work out by any means as I was often called to Granada TV, a company in Manchester, much loved by actors in those days for the terrific quality and variety of the dramatic and comedic work they produced and for the high wages they paid, accompanied on arrival in the friendly north by brown envelopes bulging with expenses and train fares in cash.

A return to theatre in the 1970s as a founder member of the irresistible, ground-breaking Actors Company (we chose the plays and offered jobs to directors) was a huge and transforming episode in my life. Sometimes we lived up to our concept of co-operative democracy, sometimes we fell short. The ideal appealed to me. It needed to. In the old-fashioned theatrical way I took my children on tour with me which was the hardest thing I have ever done. But I wouldn't have missed it for the world.

The Director of the Moscow Art Theatre, Oleg Yefremov, with his leading lady and a distinguished critic, visited Knots and Bumps, a production of ours devised by Edward Petherbridge at the Lyric Theatre, Hammersmith. I had learned a bit of Russian from an early BBC Radio course and in my eagerness to be near real Russians I invited our guests to lunch with some colleagues after which we drove to Hampton Court Palace where the leading lady wept with fear in the Maze. A genuine friendship began and they said that I would be welcome in Moscow when I was free.

It wasn't until 1982 that a week was clear to take the plunge. When the pilot announced that we had crossed the border, were flying over the Soviet Union and would soon begin our descent to Moscow, my response was disproportionate.

After I left the plane, went through customs, collected my luggage and found the taxi driver, I managed to hide for a few seconds behind a parked car so that I could kiss the ground.

Home.

C. B.

June 2011

This is the text of Black Bread and Cucumber as performed by Caroline Blakiston during 2010 to mark Anton Chekhov's 150th birthday. Certain sections from the original 1993 version were omitted, and these can be found in the Appendix on page 71.

Act I

TAGANROG

One heavy armchair, one plain wooden rehearsal chair,
one table, not more than two foot across.

The present.

> *Kremlin chimes. Caroline enters, dressed*
> *in fur hat, fur coat, fur boots etc.*

Zdrastvuitye! Dobry vyecher! OO-A! Rada Vass vidyet!

> *She starts to take off her outdoor clothes,*
> *naming them as she does so.*

Kholodna, da? Nou, pyerchatki. Shapka. Shal'. Izvenitye,
pazhaluista. Chyeryez minoutou boudou gatova. Shuba.
Ishcho shal'! Skouchna, da? Nou, shto dyelat? Vyazanaya
kofta. No, pazhaluista, razgavarivaitye! Sapagi. Gos-
padin! Rass. Vtaroi. O Bozhye moi! Rass. Vtaroi. A,
vot, na kanyets, gatova! Good evening! Worried?

That carry-on was to show you what happens when you
arrive anywhere in Russia in the middle of winter.
Whether it's an apartment, an art gallery, a cinema, a
circus, museum, restaurant, theatre – it takes five
minutes to get undressed. And, of course, it takes five
minutes to get dressed to go out into temperatures of
maybe minus ten, twenty, even thirty degrees. The

7

interiors are blessedly warm. In an apartment you'll find at least double, if not triple, glazing. We have a lot to learn from them.

Russia is a country of extremes. The cold of her winters is matched by the warmth of her people, who acknowledge and battle with dramatic opposites in their nature.

The bells you heard, which I recorded in Red Square – the chimes of the Kremlin clock – that used to control to the second the changing of the guard outside Lenin's Mausoleum, are markedly different from the stern masculine clanging of Big Ben. There's a feminine fairytale magical quality which contrasts with the rigorous discipline of the young soldiers as they performed their ritual ceremony.

I have been visiting Russia since 1982. Sightseeing, meeting actors and actresses, getting to know theatres and long-running productions. There's a production of Chekhov's The Seagull, which has been on view since before my first visit. I saw it three times in ten years – always with the same cast. And, of course, I always longed to work there.

Well, the right friend was in the right place at the right time. The astounding offer came in October 1990. I was invited to join the Dramatichesky Teatr in Taganrog, the town – on the Sea of Azov in Southern Russia – where Anton Pavlovich Chekhov was born. The play was The Cherry Orchard, the role Charlotta Ivanovna, the foreign governess, and I would, of course, be acting in Russian.

I knew at once I would accept, despite the warning of the Muscovite with whom I rush to celebrate on the telephone.

"You can't go to Taganrog, it's the provinces. You'll starve and it will be very dangerous."

I fly to Moscow to meet the Impresario and the Director. Red carnations are thrust into my hand. I decide to try out the first line of my role in Russian.

"Maya sabaka i aryekhi kushayet." (AND my dog eats nuts.)

"Your dog eats nuts?"

My confidence soars. I am driven from the airport in a converted ambulance.

That first evening the Director sits silent while the Impresario and I try to thrash out dates, finance, quality of life. I am to join the company, already a few weeks into rehearsal, on February 10th.

Back in England I have two months in which to become word perfect. It took me three days to learn that first sentence. My RADA diction exercises are of no avail as the sounds are made in a different part of the mouth. A new tongue is needed.

She practises Russian diction exercises.

Povar Pyotr povar Pavyel, Pavyel pyok, a Pyotr paril. Iz pod prigorka, iz pod pod vypod vyertyer, zaichik pripod vypod vyernulsa. Vakul babu abul, da i vakula baba abula.

9

In Moscow again the Impresario becomes the ruling personality. He is a densely built Tatar. He debunks himself almost at once by calling himself Ghengis... Ghengis Khan. He is a man of high voltage, the energy scarcely contained beneath his skin. I feel the boisterousness of his inner drive is such that he might burst like an enflamed pomegranate. Thanks to his atomic-powered determination, his ungainsayable will to creative success, I find myself making theatrical history. The first English actress to play in Chekhov in Russia in Russian. However, the clash of our personalities – call it culture shock on either side – leads us to the most ghastly rows I've ever experienced.

I feel a stubborn streak resisting him from the start. I sense he is a man who is not accustomed to asking. He is used to telling and being obeyed. The difficulty becomes clear when I offer him cigarettes from my obligatory Duty Free pack. When I move to offer to two girl assistants –

"No!"

"Why not?"

"I'm boss!"

"And I'm a person!"

... making sure they get two each. They blush with pleasure. I could hardly have flouted convention more overtly. As his employee and, even more – or less – as a woman, I have challenged him in front of his staff.

Ka - Ta - Ka - Ta   Ka - Ta - Ka - Ta   Ka - Ta - Ka - Ta

The midnight train to Taganrog – departs at 3 a.m. I travel with the Impresario and with the Administrative Director of the Dramatichesky Teatr, Vladimir Fedorovsky, a huge humorous man whom I like at once. He carries an enormous, a gigantic, Chinese thermos flask which keeps us in tea for the entire eighteen-hour journey.

In the morning I look out onto sparkling thick snow, cradling small, brightly painted wooden houses. Laden trees are like sprouting cauliflowers. A stolid couple emerges from whiteness, trudging across whiteness towards whiteness. I can see the silence that snow imposes. We are travelling due south, passing through Tula and Oryol, stations for the country estates of Tolstoy and Turgenev, the route Chekhov would have taken to Yalta in the Crimea.

"Why does the train move so slowly?"

"In order not to have an accident."

A thousand miles south of Moscow. Ten degrees below freezing. Ten-thirty at night. It hadn't occurred to me that there would be a reception party from the theatre on the platform at Taganrog. I stepped from the train to a burst of applause, smiling faces, red carnations and a formal speech of welcome in excellent English by a diminutive interpreter.

I am accompanied to the door of my room by a man with eyes bluer than his jeans. Valery. He's my night guard. After he has said 'goodnight' he reaches into his pocket and brings out a small black gun. I gasp and giggle like a schoolgirl. Then he gives me a dazzling smile. I manage to smother my second gasp. His teeth are made of gold.

The theatre in Taganrog was designed by the architect of La Scala in Milan. Built in 1866 when Chekhov was six. He saw his first performance there – La Belle Helene, by Offenbach – when he was thirteen. He used to bunk off school to be first to the top gallery to grab his favourite seat, which is marked by a medallion clearly visible from the stage.

In his day, members of the audience used to wear claque ties to show which performer they supported, so there would be competitive applause from different factions. I was told that young Anton sometimes used to add his own spice by shouting out the names of known citizens sitting in the expensive seats below him. All heads would turn to watch "MR AND MRS IVAN SMIRNOV!" blushing. It became so predictably embarrassing that some couples used to hurry out of the theatre before the clapping began rather than risk humiliation.

With scarcely time to do more than fall in love with the red, white and gold auditorium, I am led across the stage and up some stairs to a small dressing room where the rehearsal is to take place. The Director is at the table. He is a short, muscular man from Astrakhan with a beautiful bearded Emperor's head. He stands, legs apart, hands on hips, claiming his territory.

The owner of the cherry orchard, Lyuba Ranyevskaya, with her daughter Anya, the foreign governess, Charlotta Ivanovna, and a manservant, Yasha, are returning to the family home from Paris. Charlotta is an outsider. Her parents were circus people. They toured fairs. She's not a servant. She's not gentry. She doesn't fit in. During the excitement of the family arrival she is completely ignored. The Director – rightly – throws me in at the deep end with Charlotta's long speech at the beginning of Act II.

"Ou myenya nyet nastoyashova passporta. Ya nye znayou skol'ko myenya lyet, i myenye vsyo kazhyetsa shto Ya malodyenkaya. Kagda Ya byla malyenkoi dyevochkoi, to moi atyets i Mamasha yezdili po yarmarkam i davali pridstavlyenye ochyen' khoroshiye. A Ya prigala salto mortale i razniye shtuchki. I kagda Papasha i Mamasha oumirli, myenya vsyala k sibye adna Nimyetskaya Gaspazha i stala myenya ouchit'. Kharasho!"

… and then Act III, Charlotta the clown.

> *She juggles, stretches a pack of cards, and strangles herself with a silk scarf.*

I had practised some tricks and illusions… I did my whole part, except the first entrance with the dog, and I felt well supported by bold, original production.

I am, and will continue to be, three people. Zhenya is my everyday guard. The gun is handed back and forth in a sock. Sometimes I find it hiding in my handbag while she goes to fetch her son from school. I feel better about it when I discover it's loaded with gas, not bullets. The third me is my interpreter.

No matter what hints I drop about how much English people enjoy their privacy, it is not until after the last performance, a full month ahead, that I actually get to be where no-one knows I am. For fifteen minutes. These hospitable people want me to be happy all the time, and they want to witness the fact. They don't want me to feel lonely, even on the way to the lavatory.

Below the stage there is a facility for either sex. The actresses look at each other before directing me down the stairs to hell. My nose leads me. I find a girl, her hair tied back in a scarf, sweeping around a battered door behind which I can see, embedded in the ground, what had been a white china or enamel fixture with a footplate on either side. I had seen something similar in a Parisian railway station in about 1950. The pretty girl, whose job it was to keep this Augean stable clean, stepped aside charmingly.

"Je vous en prie."

... She spoke with an exquisite accent.

"Er, merci."

I am emboldened to discuss the stinky bog with Fedorovsky – not judgmentally, of course, just out of curiosity.

"How can you bear the smell?"

"We're used to it."

There's part of me, too, that welcomes the down to earth lack of pretence. In the bowels of the theatre it's the bowels which perform.

14

It's agonisingly cold. The sea is frozen so solid that people can walk out over a hundred yards. They bore holes in the ice and stand there, fishing in rows. From a distance they look like penguins. The actors huddle round the radiators.

The Director has only had five days' rehearsal on stage. He makes huge energy input, but I have misgivings about the way he plays everyone's part for them. At the break the actors go off into the dressing rooms to smoke – how they smoke! I make my way to the top gallery to sit in Chekhov's seat. I try all the nearby seats as well, in case history has made a mistake. Crazy. They're probably modern chairs.

Octavy, who plays Firs, the ancient retainer, introduces himself formally, kissing my hand. He presents me with a wrapped sweet saying, "You already have everything, so all I can give you is my heart." I frankly enjoy it. It is his little dog, Urska, who is my excited companion in the play. There is a tea party to introduce me to the rest of the actors and the theatre staff. A cake set in front of me says, in English, "Hello! May all your dreams come true!"

Kostya brings me walnuts which he cracks between his palms so that I shall get enough protein. The Literary Director – a jar of pickled cabbage. The tiny Stage Door Keeper offers apples and honey. I admire the oversized Red Army jacket she's wearing. Lilya gives me jam made out of rose petals in case I develop a sore throat. She must have got the recipe from Mount Olympus. All these nourishing homemade foods are given with such warmth that, like a well-stroked pet, I enjoy perfect health the whole time I'm in Taganrog.

February 13th. My birthday. An elaborate poster pinned to the stage door announces the fact and welcomes me. They must have looked at my passport. Shit! As I climb onto the stage – a burst of applause from the actors. All this APPLAUSE! Presents, hugging, laughter, tears. 'Happy Birthday' played on the piano by Volodya. I've been with them for three days. It already feels like three years of friendship. I expect we rehearsed a bit, too.

The Director is very fierce and rude to the actors. He shouts at them in a hectoring way. Tempers begin to rise. People answer back like anything, then laugh. It seems to me that he insults them at the core of their professionalism. He demonstrates physically, talks every point into the ground, gives line readings. How will they ever arrive at their own performance if he goes on like this?

One day he decides to change what I do at the end of the Third Act. It's an exciting new piece of business. I do it and it feels good. He tells me I haven't understood and starts to demonstrate. He does exactly what I did, but at a different moment. I call out that he's insulting me. "I know what to do, just tell me when to do it!" I can feel the pent-up frustration of the entire company being channelled through my mouth. I use his hectoring tone. I repeat myself several times. Why does he play everyone's part for them? Why doesn't he let them do their job? He looks bewildered and says he hadn't meant to insult me. Later, one of the actors takes me by the

16

hand. "We're with you!" The actresses say, "Thank you, oh thank you!"

I go down to the frozen sea and walk on the water.

I find I don't want to be separated from the other actors. I go into the girls' dressing room, needing intimacy. Like me, all four are mothers, between thirty and forty, pretty without exception, highly made up. They talk, like most of the actresses I know, of fatigue, of having no time to shop, of our children's health and school problems. But for them there is no car, nor Sainsbury's, nor even the certainty of anything worth having at the end of a three-hour queue. 'Koshmar' ('nightmare') is a popular word.

> "What can we do? We're slaves," says one of them in French.

They are apparently unresentful of the cards being so heavily stacked against them. Contrary to weary myth they are extremely feminine, and as strong as pack-horses. They laugh and laugh. But, oh how they smoke!

Lilya tells me not to stress the T at the end of words. Make them softer. First advice I've had from anyone. Very helpful. My Rs and Ts make them squeal with sympathetic laughter. "TTTURRRGENEV!" I declare to everyone I meet.

Every day for lunch I choose to eat black bread. My favourite. Black bread and cucumber.

I'm home by ten-thirty at night. Body tired, feet aching from the dancing. I get hot water for a bath by boiling huge cauldrons that I find in the kitchen. Two make the water hot enough to get into, two more top it up for another ten minutes. I have hot water from the tap not more than half a dozen times while I am in Taganrog, and I don't mind a bit. Fedorovsky laughs when I complain of the shock on the days it's there. He tells me we have been invited to give a performance of the play during the Yalta Festival in April. I already know that we are to give one in Moscow – at the Ermitage Theatre, the first home of the Moscow Art Theatre – at the end of the Taganrog run.

After my second entrance in the first half, I move to a swing upstage and stay there for the rest of the Act. About twenty minutes. I swing as discreetly as I can.

"Don't swing so discreetly. Do it more."

"If my friends in London could see me swinging while other people are trying to speak I would never live it down."

"No, no, no. If you swing sensitively to what is being said it will be like a musical accompaniment."

> She swings boldly, angrily and winsomely in turn.

I get to enjoy it and allow this unique experience to engulf me. I beg my psyche to remember. Don't let me go back to England and generalise about the Russians.

The Impresario arrives from Moscow and we do a full Dress Rehearsal – a full stopping Dress Rehearsal. He joins in the process, overriding the Director with his instructions.

March 2nd. Mr Gorbachov's birthday. Our First Night. I know that Sarah Bernhardt played in this theatre with Salvini. Vera Pantalyevna, the Dresser, is at hand to help me with my quick change. Her tenderness and love for her actors can hardly be exaggerated. She coos and soothes, using diminutives –

"Our Carolinochka our Charlottochka clever-ichka clever-ichka to talk Russian to speak Russian to act in Russian they all say how clever-ichka the actors the audience our Carolinochka nasha Carolinochka."

It's hypnotic. And as comforting as a change of nappy.

The build-up backstage is without panic. Quiet concentration. "Ni pukha ni pera," people are saying to each other. Meaning 'Neither fur nor feathers.' Their version of 'Break a leg.' "K Chortou!" goes the answer. 'To the devil!'

So the play begins. Definitely not a laughing audience to start with. Chekhov paced Charlotta wonderfully throughout the play. I did the tricks all right. The clown stuff went well. All in all, OK.

After the last scene the actors fell on each other, using their ritual phrase, "S primyeroi!" Meaning 'We've done it!' For about ten seconds I felt as if I would die of loneliness. Then I was hugged too. "S primyeroi!"

Although we had rehearsed the Curtain Call I didn't quite know what to expect. The musicians were to have played reprises of all the dance music but this was changed at the last minute to a thundering orchestral version of 'Feelings'.

> *We hear exactly that. She stands as part of an imaginary row of actors.*

"We are Noble High-Minded Artistes and you have been watching Noble High-Minded Art...

> *She takes a few steps forward.*

You may pay homage...

> *She takes a few steps back.*

... but you mustn't expect us to bow or smile."

People start to climb onto the stage from the auditorium, handing flowers to actors as well as to actresses. They are standing in the Circle as well as the Stalls and the clapping is rhythmic. I've never experienced anything quite like it in England.

> *She takes off her jacket.*

I am last to the foyer, where the party is already in full swing. I take two or three gulps of champagne on an empty stomach. Quite soon Fedorovsky gets up to make a speech, followed by one of the actors. Then I stand up.

"Ya pyanaya! I'm drunk!"

As I speak, my body floods with the realisation that I have done what I came here to do. I've actually done it. I allow myself a fiery thrust of achievement. Up go my arms in the Olympic Gold Medal gesture. "I've done it!" I yell in English.

Then Pasha, with the voice of an angel, sings to his guitar, and we pile into the theatre bus and go home.

After the final performance in Taganrog...

"Come, Carolina. Time to go home."

I sit down on the stairs.

"No. I'm not ready yet. I've been guarded for six weeks. I've given my last performance and now I'm free. I don't have to do anything I don't want to. I'm English and I'm free!"

Poor people! I decide to hide. I give them the slip and dash up to Anton's balcony, concealing myself in the Box nearest the stage.

She hides in the box.

They send out a search party. I hear them calling. I can see them.

She peers over the top of the box.

"Carolina! ... Carolinochka!! ... Nu, Carolina!!! ... Shto???"

Fifteen minutes is all I need. I go back to the foyer as if nothing had happened and allow myself to be wrapped up and taken home.

As I leave the theatre for the very last time, the Stage Door Keeper asks me to accept her Red Army jacket...

Caroline fights a ferocious internal battle then puts it on.

Ka - Ta - Ka - Ta   Ka - Ta - Ka - Ta

It's half past two in the morning. I'm on the train to Moscow. My time in Taganrog is finished. I realise this has been a very solitary experience. All the actors, all the people in Taganrog, who have responded to me with such open-hearted generosity, they all sort of have each other to discuss what it has been like to have a foreign actress working with them. The way I dress. The way I speak Russian in my funny accent. I'm the only one who knows what it feels like to be me. I don't know how to share it. I feel as if my heart will break. I'm the first foreigner to tread on the stage of that theatre for over a hundred years. It's as if Chekhov gave me permission.[1]

The day of our performance in Moscow is the day of the referendum to decide the future of the Soviet Union. Should they stay together, should they disband? I am surprised by the apparent lack of interest shown by most of my colleagues.

At the theatre I go in search of information. I see the Director and the Literary Manager sitting in an office.

"Come in! Come in!" They welcome me.

"Er, when will the dog be here?"

"Don't know."

"Well, who's arranging the dog?"

"Don't know."

"Will there be a dog?"

"No."

"No dog?"

He shrugs.

"How come the play needs a dog for twelve performances in Taganrog, but in Moscow it no longer matters?"

He laughs.

"Do I have to find a dog? Must the actress find a dog? Is it the actress's problem to find a dog? Fine. I will go out into the street and I will ask a dog if it would like to come and act with me. 'O – O – Sabachka! Khotish' igrat' sa mnoi v pyecye Chekhova?' You're not serious. You're not professional!"

I steam back to the dressing room and burst into tears of frustration.

"Surely they don't expect ME to find a dog?"

"Not serious," soothes Lyena.

Her husband, Fedorovsky, comes into the room. It's his birthday. I have given him a Mickey Mouse balloon.

"Why is she crying?"

"No dog."

"I'll deal with it."

23

A dog is found. Perfect, after one rehearsal.

During the performance, as I swing sensitively on the swing, I see the Dresser – carrying my quick-change clothes – walk unostentatiously from one side of the stage to the other in full view of the audience. No-one had shown her an alternative route!

The reception from the metropolitan audience was more enthusiastic than I had expected. The British Ambassador made a speech emphasising the European-ness of the Russians.

"What's he talking about?" said one of the actors later. "We're not European. We're Eastern."

I reflect there's some protection to be had from acting in a foreign language. The foreigner speaking my tongue has an intriguing otherness. They know they're foreign. They know I know they're foreign. Chekhov, spending a summer month at Stanislavsky's country house, made friends with a little English governess at a nearby estate. Lily Glassby. They used to play together. He gave her piggybacks. So, am I, as Charlotta, Chekhov's Englishwoman abroad?

How will he reveal himself to me as a day-to-day man in the house he built in Yalta in 1899?

Yalta church bells.

The sound of the bells of the church on the hill in Yalta sweep across the town. The similarity between this famous Crimean resort and the Côte d'Azur is

24

immediately apparent with the glistening Black Sea stretching before me.

I'm driven to the Palace Hotel, built in 1904, the year that Chekhov died. As I sign in at the desk the chic blonde receptionist asks me for which town in England I have a permit to live. Momentary collapse. Caged birds. You live where you work. You work where you live. Someone I know, who lives but is not registered in Moscow, simply pretends to be out when the police come to check his papers. I don't know how often they call.

Now that my friends have the freedom to speak their minds openly, I find myself wanting to interfere with the natural process and to prod them into taking greater steps faster. My sense of urgency on their behalf, I realise with clanging self-jolt, may be prompted by my own overdue efforts to totter towards my own freedom. Am I drawn to the Russians because we're actually in the same boat?

As I gradually assimilate new aspects of Russian life, I feel I am being handed keys to a greater understanding of Chekhov's plays. From living Russians I can learn about him. From him I can learn about them.[2]

The front door to his house carries a brass nameplate, off which A P Chekhov has almost been polished. There is a small knob – a sabachka – which...

> *We hear the tinging of Chekhov's doorbell.*

... goes like that when you twist it.

In general – I said I wouldn't generalise, but here I am – v obshchyem, Russian House Museums are faithfully decorated with reproductions of original wallpapers and hangings and, wherever possible, with actual furniture and belongings.[3]

The donkey-brown wallpaper. His worn black leather coat hanging in a glass cupboard – he was very tall. A brown canvas bag, nearly a metre wide, that had travelled with him on his six-month trip to the penal colony in Sakhalin, where he made a census of the prisoners. Imagining visits from Rachmaninov; from Chaliapin, the great bass. And Stanislavsky with his Moscow Art Theatre actors crowding to eat and drink in the dining room from which they could overflow into the glass verandah that looks down over the garden he planted himself – helps to bring the house to life. The house where he wrote his last play, The Cherry Orchard.

Outside the front door, a crowd of about a hundred have gathered in a semi-circle. A young black-bearded priest, resplendent in red Easter vestments, has come to give a blessing for the 70th anniversary of the opening of Chekhov's house as a museum.

> *Singing for the blessing of Chekhov's house.*

An informal mixed choir bursts into such happy unaccompanied harmonies that I know we really are here to celebrate.[4]

"Khristos Voskryessye! Christ is risen!"

26

The priest moves smiling around the congregation, who echo,

"Khristos Voskryessye!"

He flicks holy water with a long brush, generously and a little mischievously, in our faces as he passes.[5]

At the theatre the Taganrog actors have arrived! Family again.

Although we've been away from the play for nearly three weeks we rehearse the Second Act only. We are invited to sit in the Stalls and the Director gives his talk.

> "This is a very important performance. All the critics will be there. You must relax. And try very hard. And be at ease. You must arrive at the theatre an hour before the performance. You mustn't have anything to eat after seven o'clock. The performance begins at eight. You mustn't have anything to drink. You can drink after the performance. You may drink coffee but you mustn't have anything at all after seven o'clock..."

These are professional actors he's talking to. I can't look at him while it's going on. But they accept it, so I keep my mouth shut.[6]

What drives me – me, Caroline, to extreme feelings of outrage, is lack of information, lack of consultation, lack of choice. For want of all of these, I guess there will be a reception after the performance. It's the Yalta Festival, after all. And to this end I've put on my most extravagant party frock.

"Come quickly! They're all waiting."

Kostya has been sent to fetch the actresses. We're led to a Foyer at the Front of House. The banquettes around the walls are filled with unsmiling men and women. Including our Director. No-one moves when we appear. No-one speaks. There is not a glass of water, not a slice of bread in sight. (This is not a party.) We are not introduced. We are stared at. (This is not going to be jolly.) We sit down. A young man gets up and begins to speak.

This is a Critics' Forum. We listen to them telling each other what they think of our work. We are not addressed. We are talked about. Our Director, also being treated as an object, sits mute. I long for him to jump to his feet and challenge the bits he doesn't like. Maybe he likes it all. The actors have long since gone onto back burner. I join them enthusiastically.

Am I in such a foreign country? Is this a society which is proud of but behaves with contempt towards its creative artists, who in turn sometimes behave contemptuously towards each other? Is this what they are used to? Do they like it? Have they a choice? Who can I ask? Are we any different?

When it's over Fedorovsky approaches me about the delicate matter of my fee for the performance I have just given. I am so pleased to see him again that my spirits rise. He makes me laugh. Will he offer me less than the hundred roubles the Director intimated? Would I accept five hundred roubles? Of course. He must charge me a small amount for tax purposes. We set up a bazaar. It's delightful, Eastern, funny.

"You owe me seven roubles." (About 2 ½ p.)

I give him eight and a big hug.

"And tell me, what do you think you've come to when you are here in Russia?"

"Ooh... I believe... I believe I've come to a country that's having a nervous breakdown."

Ka - Ta - Ka - Ta

The trouble is that I am a junkie for all of this. I shall go back to England and feel exhausted and relieved and GRATEFUL and probably cry a lot. But I shall want to come back for a fix as soon as possible. A country that's having a nervous breakdown in the sense that there's no norm. Somebody will say something to you. The next minute they'll say the exact opposite with as much candour and commitment as they said the first thing – and you will see that both are true. And neither is true. So everything is improvised all the time. It's real revolution in a way. It's revolution and evolution and nobody seems to be in control of anything, I don't think, and I feel as if I'm part of an historical.... I wish I'd been alive in Chekhov's day to see if it felt like this then.

It seems to me that life consists of doing what you do from one moment to the next. That's what's happening the world over. People are simply doing what they do. At this particular moment, that's what they are doing. If you look out of the train window, people are doing what they are doing. They are walking along on their way to something, or walking back from something, or carrying a wheel, or watching us doing what we are doing, which is watching them.

The final performance with the Taganrog company is at the Vladimir International Festival. Five to seven. Two bells. One to go. I shall treasure the memory of Pasha singing to his mandolin. His melted gold musicality comically distorted by excessive vibrato.

Pasha singing.

After the curtain call I am led to the lobby. Volodya presents me with this golden amber necklace from the actors and actresses. I am invited to be their guest at a farewell party in the hotel.

When loss is imminent you attend to bodily needs: food, drink, physical closeness, music. The resourceful southerners – actors, musikanti, technicians – crowd into the little room. We interleave like sardines and eat hard-boiled eggs, tinned fish and sausage laid on bread. Each in turn records a song or a snatch to the accompaniment of Volodya or Pasha. I wish I had chosen anything but Auld Lang Syne.

In the morning Vera comes to help me pack.

"The actors are all having breakfast if you want to say one more 'Goodbye.'"

"No. No. That's the last thing I need."

One or two of them turn up and I begin to cry. Then I want to see them all. We stand in the rain. It's raining.

They climb onto the bus... I ask them to shout 'Goodbye' into my tape machine. Then they drive off to catch the train to Taganrog, where I guess I shall never set foot again.

> *From her machine the sound of the actors shouting "Dosvidanya Carolina!"*

Well, the next part of the story takes place in Moscow. I'll come back after the interval if you will!

EXIT

BLACKOUT

Above: Birthplace of Anton Chekhov, Taganrog. © Caroline Blakiston

Below: The Impresario in Moscow. © Caroline Blakiston

Above: Being greeted on arrival in Taganrog. © Caroline Blakiston

Below: The Dramatichesky Teatr in Taganrog. © Caroline Blakiston

Above: Caroline and Fedorovsky. Frozen sea, Taganrog. © Caroline Blakiston

Below: Horse and cart, Taganrog. © Caroline Blakiston

Above: Girls' dressing room, Taganrog. © Caroline Blakiston

Below: Men's dressing room, Taganrog. © Caroline Blakiston

Caroline in the dressing room, Taganrog, as Charlotta in *The Cherry Orchard*. © Caroline Blakiston

Actors of the Taganrog Theatre Company. © Caroline Blakiston

Clockwise from top left: Pasha; Octavy, with his dog Urska; Kostya; and Lev.

Above: The Moscow Art Theatre. © Caroline Blakiston

Below: Oleg Yefremov, director of the Moscow Art Theatre until his death in 2000. © Caroline Blakiston

Above: Laying flowers for Yevstignyeyev outside Moscow Art
Theatre. © Caroline Blakiston

Below left: The poster advertising Caroline's appearance in
Moscow. © Caroline Blakiston

Below right: Statue of Chekhov outside the Moscow Art Theatre
© Pablo Sanchez

Rehearsing at Moscow Art Theatre. © Caroline Blakiston

Above, L-R: Andrey Davidov, Caroline, Petya Shcherbakov and Polina Medvedyeva.

Below, L-R: V. Nyevinny, Borya Shcherbakov, Petya, V. Sergachov, and Andrey.

Above left: Smokhtunovsky dropping hints in rehearsal.
Above right: Script of *The Cherry Orchard*, Moscow Art Theatre.
Below left: Nyevinny and Henrietta.
Below right: Charlotta, Act III, Moscow Art Theatre.
All © Caroline Blakiston

ДѢЙСТВІЕ ВТОРОЕ (2)

~~Так хочется поговорить, а не о кем... Никого у меня нет.~~
(Выстрелила зонтиком.) Кончила. Теперь пойду. Ты, Епиходов, очень умный человекъ и очень страшный: тебя должны безумно любить женщины. Брррр! Так хочется поговорить, а не о кем... Никого у меня нетъ.

ДѢЙСТВІЕ ТРЕТЬЕ (2)

ПИЩИКЪ (удивляясь). Вы подумайте! Очаровательнѣйшая Шарлотта Ивановна... я просто влюбленъ...

ШАРЛОТТА. Влюбленъ? (Пожавъ плечами.) Развѣ вы можете любить? *Guter Mensch, aber schlechter Musikant.*

ТРОФИМОВЪ (хлопаетъ Пищика по плечу). Лошадь вы этакая...

ШАРЛОТТА. Прошу вниманія, еще одинъ фокусъ. (Беретъ со стола плэдъ.) Вотъ очень хорошій плэдъ, я желаю продавать... (Встряхиваетъ.) Не желаетъ ли кто покупать?

ПИЩИКЪ (удивляясь). Вы подумайте!

ШАРЛОТТА. Айнъ, цвай, драй! (Быстро поднимаетъ опущенный плэдъ; за плэдомъ стоитъ Аня, она дѣлаетъ реверансъ, бѣжитъ къ матери, обнимаетъ ее и убѣгаетъ назадъ въ залу при общемъ восторгѣ.)

ЛЮБОВЬ АНДРЕЕВНА (аплодируетъ). Браво, браво!..

ШАРЛОТТА. Теперь еще! Айнъ, цвай, драй. (Поднимаетъ плэдъ; за плэдомъ стоитъ ВАРЯ и кланяется.)

ПИЩИКЪ (удивленно). Вы подумайте!

ШАРЛОТТА. Конецъ! (Бросаетъ плэдъ на Пищика, дѣлаетъ реверансъ и убѣгаетъ въ залу.)

ПИЩИКЪ (спѣшитъ за ней). Злодѣйка... какова? Какова? (Уходитъ.)

Page from the script of *The Cherry Orchard*, Moscow Art Theatre.

Above: Costume fitting at Moscow Art Theatre. © Caroline Blakiston

Below: With Sasha and Ksenia in their Moscow flat. © Caroline Blakiston

Curtain call at Moscow Art Theatre with Smokhtunovsky.
© G. Nesmachny

Above and below: In *Black Bread & Cucumber* at the Orange Tree Theatre in 1993. © AMRON

Act II

MOSCOW ART THEATRE

> *Caroline enters to a rock version of The Red Flag.*

The coup which dislodged Mikhail Gorbachov during the late teens of August 1991 appears not to have interfered with the telephone service. I dial Moscow as usual.

0107 095...

"Are you all right?"

"Yes, of course."

"What are you doing?"

"We go to work as usual. When are you coming back?"

"Don't know."

"Shall we see if Oleg Yefremov will invite you to play in his production of The Cherry Orchard in MXAT?"

"Yes!"

MXAT! Moskovsky Khudozhestvyeny Akademichesky Teatr. [*Caroline points to a random person in the audience.*] You say it! ...... MXAT. Moscow Art Theatre.

In 1897 a distinguished playwright, director and teacher, Vladimir Nemirovich-Danchenko sent a note to a young merchant, Konstantin Stanislavsky, suggesting a meeting at a favoured Moscow eating house, Slavyanski Bazaar. This privileged young businessman had made a name for himself as an unusually talented amateur actor and director. His family firm, under their real name Alexeyev, manufactured – amongst other things – gold thread, but he had an interest in forming a fully professional theatre company. He was tall, handsome and rich. Their encounter started at 2 p.m. on 22nd June and continued for eighteen hours. They moved from the restaurant, drove to Stanislavsky's country estate, Lyubimovka, outside Moscow. They talked through the night and by eight o'clock the following morning the Moscow Art Theatre had been conceived.

The association between these two men, sometimes a sticky one, lasted – endured – for more than forty years. Their company soon gained a huge reputation for the excellence of its innovative work and it still lives and works in the building that was designed for them by Shek'tel over a hundred years ago in the Art Nouveau style that was so popular at the beginning of the last century. Inside the auditorium there's a linear design, olive green and beige.

Oleg Nikolayevich Yefremov has been in charge of the Moscow Art Theatre for around twenty years. He is Artistic Director, director of plays, star actor and the Russian theatre man I have known longer than any other.

I will be more likely to entice set dates from him if we are face to face in a room. I'd better get over there.

In their snowy capital, while awaiting the summons to MXAT, I have dinner with two close friends to discuss another project which we hope to present to Russian and to English audiences. We eat and bring ourselves up to date.

"Have you had your meeting with Yefremov?"

"No, not yet."

We try to cut through the fantasies we have about each others' national artistic imperatives.

"I can see that, governmentally, you are seriously pushed for money, but I believe your innate cultural thrust is towards high-minded adventurous activity."

"Wrong!" they shout joyously. "We are a nation of stupid, ignorant arseholes with no interest in anything but money and vodka."

Russian actors express themselves quite freely.

"No, no, we must definitely do it in England. Is there any way that YOU can raise some finance for this sort of project?"

"Finance?" I screech. "They can't finance books for schoolchildren. No, no, no. We are a nation of scornful, insular arseholes with no interest in anything except money and scandal."

English actresses express themselves quite freely.

We get all of that out of the way.

The next day – ignition!   Irina, Yefremov's assistant, takes charge.

> "Oleg is away at the moment but he wants us to fix dates so that we can make announcements and plan publicity. Now, you will need two rehearsals."

> "Only two?"

> "Let's go and see Tanya. She arranges these things."

Tanya is as glamorous as any of the actresses in the company and turns out to be one of the actresses in the company.   She has to accommodate nearly seventy artists, there are usually several productions in rehearsal at any one time and no play is given more than two consecutive performances.

> *She consults her schedule.*

> "Now, you will need two rehearsals."

> "Only two?"

> "And one on stage."

Only one? But not out loud. I have become a Lilliputian in the face of these potentials. I leave her office with two rehearsals, plus one on stage, and two performances pencilled in for the second week in March, three months away.

I ask for a copy of the play, as I know that the text for the Second Act is a little different from the one we used in

Taganrog. It's not that I have to learn any new lines, but imagine singing the notes of The Blue Danube in a different order.

She does.

I can watch a performance of the production I shall be joining, conveniently scheduled for the night before I leave Moscow. I am invited to come for a costume fitting an hour before curtain up. They really do mean business.

Backstage the theatre is as meticulously designed as the front of house. Stanislavsky believed in the dignity of actors and insisted on first-class accommodation for them. The main staircase to the dressing rooms is rather wide and grand, made of classic marble. The dressing room itself is stylishly laid out in the original way. The actors are treated to the same blond wood panelling, doors and chairs as the audience. The neat dressing table has four small standard lamps on it.

Putting on tailcoat.

"Come and meet Tenyakova, who plays Ranyevskaya."

Moving towards Tenyakova's dressing room.

"This is Carolina, who will be playing Charlotta Ivanovna."

"Tonight?"

"Oh heavens, no! In March, I hope."

"Good, good. Till we meet, then."

March 12th is the day of my first rehearsal. It's the anniversary of my last performance in Taganrog. There are no accidents. The postcode for Taganrog – 347900 – almost exactly matches my Equity number – 34970. Accident? Please!

>*Starts to tie pink silk scarf round her neck.*

These actors – the cast consists of the equivalent of five Knights, one Dame and three CBEs – they have been playing in this production for nearly three years. I hope they'll feel friendly towards me. I wear pale pink.

Henrietta – Genrietta – they use G for H. Hamlet – Gamlet. Gitler...... Henrietta, a long-standing Russian friend, has agreed to be my unofficial interpreter, leaving her perilously ill mother in Sebastopol in the Crimea, now part of the Ukraine. She tells how a group of nationalist Ukrainians have clamoured for the Russians there to go home. 'The Crimea has been reclaimed!' It's meaty stuff for unionists who fear the thunderclap of nationalism with violence. A demonstration in Moscow has been planned – and banned by President Yeltsin and Mayor Popov – for the day of the first anniversary of that referendum I talked about in the first half (when they actually voted to disband the Soviet Union). The old guard will try to persuade the Deputies to put Humpty Dumpty together again. We are promised two hundred and fifty thousand activists, tanks on the streets, barricades...

I have asked Henrietta whether, before meeting me, she can possibly buy me two or four carnations. Flowers, in even numbers, are given when someone has died. I know that MXAT has recently lost one of its most distinguished actors, Yevstignyeyev, and I want, as my first gesture in his theatre, to give Oleg Yefremov flowers in memory of this glorious performer, whom I had often watched. Henrietta tells me that even more recently another actor from a different branch of MXAT has died.

"There'll be a third."

I voice the superstition that theatrical deaths come in threes.

Henrietta looks sideways at Caroline.

Is Carolina a witch?

The first actor to arrive at rehearsal is tall magnificent Andrey, who plays Yasha, Ranyevskaya's smartypants manservant. He is wearing a smart striped suit and his friendly welcome is given in suave American English. This actor excels at playing the weaving drunk butler.

Heavy drinking is rather rare for actors and actresses in England. It is largely disapproved of. So drunk acting is something that has to be learned like a foreign body language. In Russia, my impression is, everybody KNOWS how to drink. I mean DRINK, in a courageous, sustained, continuous, lasting way. Not in the "Two glasses of champagne and I'm anybody's!" style which afflicts me. Both men and women appear to me to have a prodigious capacity for alcohol. They can talk and even listen and engage in convincing argument with half a bottle of vodka inside every belly around the table. I watch it with awe. It's a tourist attraction for me.

One man I met a few times has a punishing attitude to drink. I watch him perform a ritual. He cuts an apple into small pieces. Empties a brimming glass of vodka. The first breath he takes after swallowing is inhaled through a piece of apple which he holds tight against his nostrils.

She demonstrates.

Then he eats the morsel. This format enables him to keep on drinking. The fumes from vodka are disagreeable. It is drunk for the result, not for the taste. Hangovers are largely unacknowledged. Maybe it's a question of habit. They're used to drinking... We're used to hiding our feelings... Well, we were until the last day of August, 1997...

"Carolina!"

The warm bass voice of Oleg Nikolayevich Yefremov. I turn to see my old friend, now my employer, flanked by two assistants. He always has a superb haircut. Some days he looks tall, others less so. His actor's hands are clear and to the point. He welcomes me to the theatre [*he kisses her hand*], accepts the flowers in memory of Yevstignyeyev, says a few words to complete the little ceremony, then moves to the Director's position by the table.

"Well, do what you want to do. She has her own tricks. Let her do what she wants."

"But Oleg... it's your production..."

"No, no, no, feel free. Do anything you like. I'm sorry I can't stay. I have to go to another rehearsal."

And off he goes!"

"You will see him on Monday," Kolya hastens to reassure me. "He will be at the Dress Rehearsal on the morning of your first performance."

The actors in rehearsal are exactly what I wanted them to be. Helpful and funny. Petya Shcherbakov, Uncle Petya, plays Simeonov-Pishchik, the only character in the play who responds generously and personally to Charlotta. He is a flustered, worried, adoring neighbour of Ranyevskaya. He is kindness itself, inclined to fall asleep without warning. This smiling actor agrees at once when I ask him to help me with a card trick to surprise the others, one which is not usually part of the production.

Another handsome giant bounds into the room, bursting with energy and juice. Shkalikov, who plays Trofimov, the serious eternal student. This actor's personality is engagingly subversive. He starts to play with Charlotta's prop dog, doing a double act with Shcherbakov.

> *Prop dog lifts leg against trouser to disgust of recipient.*

Suddenly I see Innokenti Mikhailovich Smokhtunovsky, the acknowledged Grand Master of Russian actors – in the 1960s film, the most revealing Hamlet I have seen – sitting, legs crossed, chin cupped in his left hand, leaning sideways over the back of a wooden chair. A smile plays gently. Smokhtunovsky was a man unlike any other I have met. His presence was astonishingly light. Airy. Weightless, almost. Spiritual. I felt I could invite him to step onto my finger and lift him as high as I will. His thespian face was territory over which battles had been fought and won. He stood to welcome me [*he kisses her hand*], and we began to rehearse the family return at the beginning of Act I. Smokhtunovsky played Gaev, Ranyevskaya's feckless, billiard-miming brother.

Smokhtunovsky soon took the lead in my schooling. He was a most delicate man. He dropped hints, made suggestions about the role, the play, the author. Then immediately seemed to retract in case it was an intrusion. He put his finger to his lips as if asking for silence. Bent his head inquiringly like a robin.

The Yefremov production has Charlotta distract attention from the fact that she has refused to do a party trick to order by pointing out the bad habit of smoking.

> *Charlotta takes a box of matches from her pocket, extracts a cigarette stub and lights it.*

She removes the cigarette from Ranyevskaya's mouth.

"Nye nada!"

Charlotta looks around, takes a handkerchief from Lopakhin's pocket, shows it front and back to the assembled company, lays it over her left hand and proceeds with the disappearing cigarette illusion.

"Carolinochka! Mozhno pozhaluista. One more little suggestion. May I? Maybe? Maybe not?"

Act III was always my favourite in Taganrog, and so it is here. I feel indescribably happy in my Clown costume. The unpredictable, magical, somewhat dangerous side of Charlotta can take hold. She moves into an androgynous world. Man? Woman? Both? Neither? She can draw on the extremes of each. Cruel or compassionate, without warning or justification. Free to show all the grief she has ever known. All the joy. It is a seductive habitat.

I used to fear clowns when I was taken to the Circus as a child. Those great painted papier-mâché heads filled me with dread. ("Please, God, don't let us have seats in the front row or the aisle.") The Clown without the extra head is even worse. His face is painted to make me feel sorry for him. He's tearful and vulnerable. But allow him close and he could show savage heartlessness. He might peer deep into my soul with the small wet eyes that sit behind the exaggerated make-up and command me to stand up in the blinding searchlight that follows him around. ("Please, God, don't let him come this way.")

I knew my need to be an actress before I was eight. That was after I decided not to be a choirboy.

"Caroline wants to be an actress. She'll help the conjuror." ("No, God, please God, no.")

I rooted in paralysed unending blush, eyes welling, while a man dressed in black and white said:

"Here is an umbrella and here is a sheet of newspaper. What shall I do with them?" ("Why is he asking me? Doesn't he know how to do the trick? Please, God, don't let the tears run over until I'm sitting down again.")

He tried again, showing his audience with a look that he had chosen his assistant badly. My mind blanked out by shame and terror I waited for the agony to end.

"Wrap them up," he prompted eventually, seeing he had a flop on his hands.

"Wrap them up," I whispered.

"Any anxieties? Any worries?" Kolya asks me kindly at the end of the second day's rehearsal.

"No. No. Well, yes... I need more rehearsal."

"You will remember everything. No problem."

When I am in Moscow I live with Sasha and Ksenia. In their home the normality of domesticity helps to cool the rising barometer of creativity. They are a devout couple. Lent is experienced fully in churchgoing and fasting. Ksenia comes home one day, gleeful at having succeeded in buying fresh yeast. This is crumbled onto a tray in the kitchen and left to dry on the windowsill above the radiator. It will stay there, a temptation to straying, playing fingers, until she comes to make her Easter cakes for the family. I know one or two homes in Moscow and in southern Russia where photographs of the last Tsar are displayed alongside religious icons.

In this comfortable third-generation apartment I find myself wondering about the Revolution. I wish I knew how many people were involved. I can't picture it in numbers. Would they constitute a full house at Wembley?

I am entrusted with a set of keys to their apartment. The recent growth in crime means that everyone is having extra locks and bolts fitted to their doors. It becomes quite a procedure to get in. If the little sabachka on the inside is facing the wrong way, you can't get in. Something has to be done. A locksmith has to be called. It speaks ill of my Western conditioning that I feel even a flicker of surprise that a locksmith can be called. But people have been living in Moscow getting things done for years. For years and years and years. Since 1147, in fact.

For my one rehearsal on stage on Saturday half the set has been wheeled into place. I am given full cast, full lighting, full orchestra.

I am granted an extra four hours on my own in a room on Sunday afternoon, with a soufflyor, a specialist prompter. She patiently reads all the other parts while I repeat my entrances and exits. I practise the tricks – using her body as stooge – and we both make sure that Charlotta gives the music cues correctly.

"I feel so happy and excited!" I blurt to Isolde as I pass her table in the canteen.

She spits delicately three times over her left shoulder. It's common practise. It's the equivalent of crossing your fingers for luck.

I make my way down to the stage. Bare. Abandoned, after a matinee. I go to the prompt corner and find a chair. I take it to the front of this famous, famous stage. In my own time I will get the feel. I will find my position of command. I send my message systematically to every seat in the auditorium... After a while some technicians, wearing soundproof felt slippers, come to change the rods that hold the black velvet drapes. We exchange friendly nods. It's very warm. After an hour or so I take some photographs. I pick up some splinters from the bare boards. They'll make good First Night presents for very special people who understand about my Russian illness.

I spend the evening before my premiere wrapping small presents and writing cards to thank the actors for their help and encouragement.

I wake to a bright morning. The snow on the branches of the trees in the courtyard below is icing sugar. As I gently negotiate entry into this climactic, dream of a lifetime day, I have time to open my pores and strengthen myself with the ordinariness of some of my recent experiences. I must be looking to some degree native as I am stopped in the street by a young man asking the way to the Moscow Art Theatre Studio.

"I'm going that way myself."

Or a very dishevelled out-of-town old man. "Is it this way? Is this the way?" I couldn't make out what or where.

"I'm sorry. I don't know. Izvinitye, pozhaluista, Ya nye znayou. Ya Anglichanka."

"Nichivo, nichivo." He forgave me, laughing.

Or I might bump into someone I know – like Slava Lyubshin. Film star, heart-throb, on his way to give a performance of Tartuffe at the Moscow Art...

... at MY theatre.

He pulled the collar of my coat closer round my neck.

"You must keep warm. It's very cold."

He was dressed in jeans and ski hat like any other passing worker. No question of presenting himself starrily in the street to be recognised. I suppose it's hard to preen in four inches of slush.

Events. Events take charge. I arrive at the theatre to prepare for the Dress Rehearsal.

"We have great sorrow. Shcherbakov has died in the night."

Shcherbakov? Simeonov-Pishchik? Uncle Petya? Not an old man. The third actor dies. A friendly co-operative colleague, with whom I have scarcely brushed wings, has called it a day. I understand at once that this is a family loss for the theatre.

In my warm cheerful dressing room, little Tanya appears with removing cream and hairbrush. I can see that no commiseration will be adequate.

"Perhaps they'll cancel the performance?"

"No. No. Everything is going ahead. Oleg Yefremov has been in the theatre since nine o'clock, rehearsing with Kashpur. He will learn the lines and go on tonight."

"No understudy?"

"No."

She flies down the passage.

Wearing my costume I go down to the stage where I see several of the actors standing about, inert, invaded by the news. I see others being pole-axed as they arrive. Polina, sitting at the bottom of the stairs. Wiped out.

"I'm with you."

Polina nods, speechless.

They are all open, affectionate, hurt. Tenyakova, completely overwhelmed. Nyevinny, one of the widest men I have ever met – and one of the nimblest – can hardly speak. But they hug. Everyone hugs me. And I hug them. It's an extraordinary... It's an archetypal theatrical happening, a death. We go on anyway. There's no business like show business. Kashpur hurries onto the stage. Kisses, hugs me.

A table has been set up in the Stalls for Oleg Yefremov. His glass of tea and his ashtray ready. As he enters the auditorium, very formal – "Let's begin. Let's begin." I can see that he must do a full Dress Rehearsal. He must do the whole play for the new Simeonov-Pishchik, for Kashpur. Not just my scenes.

After my first line and exit I stand in the wings. Tenyakova indicates a chair for me to sit on.

"I'm fine, thanks."

"Sit down! Sit down. I'M TELLING YOU!"

She takes my hand, fiercely kind. Everything is going to be heightened today.

On stage Shkalikov is being practical. He leads Kashpur from place to place. Gradually the atmosphere relaxes. The actors begin to be able to hear each others' attempts at jokes and to laugh a little. The possibility of future re-enters the arena. Russian adaptability. It takes the pressure off. The feeling that we're going to survive anyway stops the over-dramatic do or die sensationalism. It will be all right. We'll improvise. It's the Russian credo. It's what they're made for. It's what they're in training for all the time. There is no better way to demonstrate it.

An unforeseen demand comes at the end of the Fourth Act. The family are preparing to say farewell to their home for the very last time. Wearing their outdoor clothes, they're sitting for a while before leaving. It's the Russian habit. Simeonov-Pishchik arrives in a flurry to pay back some money he owes. He is unaware that a major departure is at hand. When it hits him he, too, on the verge of tears, sits – in this production – on the family rocking horse. He says:

> "Well, there we are... There we are... Be happy... God give you strength... There we are, then. To everything in this world there is an end... And if one day you should hear a rumour that the end has come for me, then remember... this old horse, and say: 'Once on this earth there was a certain Simeonov-Pishchik... God rest his soul...'"

Kashpur, reading from the script, bravely keeps going. Many of the actors begin to cry. Nyevinny, sitting there, huge, sweating. His great wounded face suddenly streams with unconsolable tears. The actors look at the ground. They look anywhere rather than at the rocking horse where their friend had sat.

In the evening three bells, two bells, one bell signify the decreasing time to curtain up, as in Taganrog.

In the first short scene debutants Kashpur and I get our bearings. In the second the Disappearing Cigarette disappears. I have quite a long wait before the final entrance. I am joined by Smokhtunovsky. He asks whether I would like to sit down. Terrified of missing my cue I decline. He stays beside me.

> "It's not really a very good day to have your premiere."

> *Caroline nods agreement.*

He begins to talk quietly about a film he made in Italy with "One of your great stars..."

64

I think I hear silence on stage. I've missed it! I dash forward.

"No, no, no, no. Not yet, not yet." He saves me. "You're far too early. There's plenty of time. Ages."

"A week?"

"A month."

After the curtain call the actors, emptied of everything, hug me and go away to grieve. Suddenly, there is Oleg Yefremov. A tear sits in the corner of his eye and I know that the time has come for me to allow my own feelings to overflow.

"Congratulations," he says, gently.

In bed that night I do dozens of re-runs of A Day In The Life Of An English Actress. I stop when I get to a frame that tells me that I neither wrapped a present nor wrote a card for Uncle Petya Shcherbakov. Only for him did I not.

Funeral music.

The funeral of Petya Shcherbakov in the theatre at noon. I am not sure whether my presence will be appropriate. It might be intrusive. I'll just have to judge that when I get there. I need to be with them. I carry four carnations.

Inside the stage door all the actors and the theatre staff are assembled, wearing black. I've managed to find a black skirt but I have no dark top. I begin to feel self-conscious. I shall have to put my thick black overcoat on again. The attendant can't understand why I am leaving before the ceremony. I explain my predicament.

> *The attendant peels off her own purple cardigan.*

"Will this do?"

"Thank you. Oh thank you very much."

In the auditorium the lights are at half strength. I am astonished to see three or four hundred people sitting in the Stalls. The doors to the street have been unlocked and passers-by are coming in and paying their last respects in company with the theatre family.

A huge blown-up photograph of Petya Shcherbakov hangs against black velvet drapes at the back of the stage. A small mourning curtain is swathed across one corner. In the centre of the dimly lit stage, tilted up on a raised dais, rests the coffin which holds the embalmed body of the actor. Three rows of chairs are set a few yards from the coffin on either side. On these sit family mourners, Yefremov, Smokhtunovsky and other senior actors.

Solemn music is playing. It is a concentration of devotion and regret.

The widow, a small black lace shawl covering her head, is leaning over her husband. She seems to be talking to him. The intimacy of a domestic relationship is being brought to a close in public.

Yefremov is speaking as I join a queue which leads to steps up onto the stage. I ask my neighbour...

"What shall I do?"

"You walk up and lay your flowers and stay for a while."

The only embalmed face I had looked at previously had been that of Lenin, behind glass, so I am not at all shocked. But I am thoroughly upset. To my left Mrs Shcherbakov is being given, like a child, sips from a small glass by a young woman. She maintains a low, moaning sob. My own tears run down my neck into my borrowed cardigan.

Yefremov rises from time to time to introduce a speaker. Some of the Cherry Orchard actors try. Shkalikov's voice breaks as he struggles to get his words out. Smokhtunovsky is the last to speak. He draws his palm across his forehead as if to wipe away the pain. Wrings his hands repeatedly. When he has finished, many of the mourners hurry up onto the stage again. The actors go back to have a last look. Some of them kiss Uncle Petya. They loved him.

I've never seen anything like it. It's theatre. There is a large compliant audience. I can't imagine such a scene in England. I feel completely at home here. Ya zdyess doma.

Before my third and last – I was given one extra performance – I am visited in my dressing room by people coming to give me little presents. To say goodbye.

I dissolve.

"I'm sorry... I can't..."

They back out, horrified at having upset me. In bounds Shkalikov.

"Carolinochka…"

I start to sob.

"Carolinochka, we're going to make an announcement before the performance that we have said goodbye to our friend today."

I sob and sob.

"Carolinochka, don't cry… Everything will be all right… Please don't cry… Darling Carolinochka… It will be all right."

Off he goes.

I can't stop. I can't stop. I'm not going to be able to get down to the stage. I'm not going to be able to speak. I'll have to find something to frighten myself with.

Miss Medley's disapproving voice as she read the notices at supper a few days before I played Darcy in the school production of Pride and Prejudice. My shoulder-length hair had been cut to an approximation of Jane Austen's hero and the result was there for the whole school to see.

"Will the girl who left a pile of hair in the French Aural Examination room kindly come and see me in the Staff Room after supper."

Just before the end of the play Charlotta has to beg for a job from Lopakhin, the man who, by buying the cherry orchard, has put her out of work.

"Tak vy, pozhaluista, naiditye mnye myesta. Ya nye magou tak."

Borya, playing Lopakhin, contacted strongly with me in this moment. He took a huge step sideways and turned his back to the audience so that none of the attention should be on him. It's the most graciously noble gesture I've ever encountered on stage... until the curtain call... when Smokhtunovsky led the rest of the actors off stage, leaving me there alone......

'May all your dreams come true.'

So I got to Moscow.

Oh, Three Sisters...

Olga. Masha. Irinochka.

Eat your hearts out!

Do svidanya, i spassibo.

She leaves.

BLACKOUT

THE END

APPENDIX

The following passages appeared in the original 1994 production of Black Bread and Cucumber, but have since been deleted.

1   On the train I walk up and down the corridor to get a bit of exercise, to loosen my limbs. It's an eighteen-hour journey to Moscow. There's a bar at exactly the right height for – if you were a dancer you could – it's to stop you falling over if the train wobbles – it's exactly the right height to do your exercises.

> *She uses the back of the wooden chair as a barre.*

[Page 22]

2   Walking uphill towards his house I pass a road sign PAVEMENT. Unnecessary for the sighted. No use to the blind.

[Page 25]

3   The wish to satisfy the voracious tourist can lead to a 'unique' picture being on view in more than one place. I have found myself asking, "Haven't I seen this portrait in another museum?"

"Oh yes, that is the original. This is a copy."

[Page 26]

4   A young disabled boy, twelve or fourteen – an elf – is exploring the crowd. He stares up into my face for

several minutes. He doesn't speak. He is given holy passage.

[Page 26]

5   The elf, carrying a lighted candle, has place of honour in the procession that follows the priest back into the house to disrobe.

[Page 27]

6   The audience are a little stiff to start with, but the laughs come in the customary places. "Loud and fast!" encourages Pasha. The actors' password.

[Page 27]

The end of the play was also changed in 2010. The original ending was as follows:

Well, that's it. I've done what I wanted to do...

Eat your heart out, Napoleon!

She laughs and leaves.

PHOTO CREDITS

Page 4 Caroline on stage as Charlotta in *The Cherry Orchard* at the Moscow Art Theatre in 1992. © Yuri Gripas

Page 6 Russia in Winter. © Caroline Blakiston

Page 70 Curtain call at the Moscow Art Theatre. © G. Nesmachny

Page 75 Caroline Blakiston. © John McKay

AUTHOR BIOGRAPHY

Caroline Blakiston is an award-winning RADA-trained actress who has taken many leading roles in theatre, film and television.

She was a founder member of the Actors Company, and played two seasons with the Royal Shakespeare Company, during which she played Volumnia in *Coriolanus*, Cornelia in *The White Devil*, Philaminte in *The Learned Ladies* and Mistress Overdone in *Measure for Measure*. Her recent theatre credits include Lady Markby in *An Ideal Husband*, Mrs Higgins in Trevor Nunn's production of *My Fair Lady* and Lady Pontefract in Adrian Noble's *A Woman of No Importance*. In 1987 she won the Charrington Best Actress award for her performance in Martin Allen's *Particular Friendships*, directed by Michael Attenborough. In 1968 she created the role of Cynthia Muldoon in Tom Stoppard's *The Real Inspector Hound* at the Criterion Theatre.

In 1991 Caroline became the first English actress to play in Chekhov in Russia in Russian, as Charlotta Ivanovna in *The Cherry Orchard*, which she first performed in Chekhov's birthplace, Taganrog, and then, in 1992, at the Moscow Art Theatre. In 1994 she won the Golden Globe Award for her special contribution to Russian theatre. It was from these experiences that Caroline created her one-woman entertainment, *Black Bread and Cucumber*, which she has subsequently taken around the world, and last performed at the Jermyn Street Theatre in 2010 in celebration of Chekhov's 150th birthday.

Recent television credits include episodes of *Midsomer Murders*, *Doctors* and *Heartbeat*, Lady Partridge in *The Line of Beauty*, Judith Villiers in *Children of the New Forest* and

Lionel's ex-wife Margaret in the popular sitcom *As Time Goes By*. Other parts include: Lady Patience Hardacre in three series of the satirical comedy *Brass* opposite Timothy West; Scarlett in taxi drama *Rides*; Lady Bess Sedgwick in *Miss Marple: At Bertram's Hotel* with Joan Hickson; the Co-ordinator in *Mr Palfrey of Westminster*; Margaret Mottram in Keith Waterhouse's *Charters and Caldicott*; Alice Bannister in Carla Lane's *The Last Song*; Anna Brigmore in *The Mallens*; Kathleen Fenton QC in *Crown Court*; Lady Harriet in *Wives and Daughters*; Agrippina in *The Caesars* and Marjorie Ferrar in the original *Forsyte Saga*. She also appeared in many cult Sixties series such as *The Saint, Randall and Hopkirk (Deceased), The Baron, The Champions, Department S* and *The Avengers*.

Her film credits include: the White Nun in *The Trygon Factor*; Hon. Esther Grand in *The Magic Christian*; *Sunday Bloody Sunday*; *Yanks*; Angela Berenson in *The Fourth Protocol*; Margaret Thatcher in *Coup!*; Mrs Quincy in *Scoop*; and leader of the Rebel Alliance, Mon Mothma, in *Star Wars: Return of the Jedi*.